2401 OBJECTS

Written by Hannah Barker, Lewis Hetherington and Liam Jarvis
Devised by the company

Additional text drawn from transcripts of telephone interviews
with Dr Jacopo Annese

An Analogue, Oldenburgisches Staastheater
and New Wolsey Theatre co-production

2401 Objects was first performed at Oldenburgisches Staatstheater, Germany on 17 June 2011. The UK premiere was at Pleasance Courtyard, Edinburgh on 3 August 2011.

Cast and Devising Team
in order of appearance

DR JACOPO ANNESE / HENRY MOLAISON	Sebastien Lawson
PATIENT HM / FATHER	Pieter Lawman
NURSE / LAUREN / MOTHER	Melody Grove
STAGE MANAGER	Helen Mugridge

Creative and Production Team

Directors	Liam Jarvis and Hannah Barker
Text	Lewis Hetherington
Producer	Ric Watts
Set Designer	Anike Sedello
Lighting Designer	Alexander Fleischer
Sound Designer	Alexander Garfath
Multimedia Designer	Thor Hayton
Dramaturgical Support	Jörg Vorhaben
Production Managers	Helen Mugridge and David Sherman
Technician	Max Wingate
Assistant Director	Katharina Wisotzki
Assistant Designer	Markus Wagner
Set and Costumes	Built and made by Oldenburgisches Staatstheater
Press Representative	Mobius Industries
Primary Research Consultant	Dr Jacopo Annese, The Brain Observatory, San Diego
Research Consultants	Professor John Aggleton, University of Cardiff, Hanna Pickard, Oxford Centre for Neuroethics, Heather Rea, Edinburgh Beltane Beacon for Public Engagement, Christopher Stock, Jen Middleton and P Bowers, The Wellcome Trust.

An Analogue, Oldenburgisches Staatstheater and New Wolsey Theatre co-production.

Developed at Farnham Maltings, National Theatre Studio and Jacksons Lane.

Supported by Wellcome Trust, Royal Holloway University, Arts Council England, Escalator East to Edinburgh and British Council Germany.

Supported by

LOTTERY FUNDED

We'd like to thank the following people who have made this project possible: Everyone at Oldenburgisches Staatsheater, especially Jörg Vorhaben, Markus Müller, Thomas Kraus, Tilmann Pröllochs, Alexander Fleischer, Oliver Eck, Markus Wagner and Katharina Wisotzki. Everyone at The New Wolsey Theatre, Ipswich, especially Sarah Holmes, Pete Rowe, and Rob Salmon. Gavin Stride and Fiona Baxter at Farnham Maltings. Purni Morell, Gareth Machin, Matthew Poxon and Tarek Iskander at National Theatre Studio. Adrian Berry and all at Jacksons Lane. Jenny Paton, Rosie Tooby and all at The Wellcome Trust. All at Arts Council England. Anthony Roberts and the Escalator East to Edinburgh team. Tony Greenwood, Lydia Daniels, Martin Kelly and Royal Holloway University for their unwavering support. Everyone at the Pleasance, especially Cassandra Mathers. Dan Ford, Katie Underwood, Matt Tait, Neal Craig, Sarah Belcher, Tommy Luther and Mark Healy for taking part in early workshops on the show. Dan Pursey and Amber Massie-Blomfield at Mobius. Andrew Walby and everyone at Oberon. Our scientific consultants who have made valuable contributions to our research. Also, The Barker Family, Geoff Monaghan, Lesley, Colin & Hayley Jarvis, John & Gill Grieve, Helen Cooper, Alex Markham, Simon Bedford, Chris Woodley, Dan Rebellato, Emma Jowett, Dan Tobin, Sam Taylor and all of those who continue to contribute emotionally, psychologically and financially to the company and this project.

ANALOGUE

Analogue is a South East-based company that makes visceral new theatre. Our multidisciplinary process fuses the high-tech with the low-tech, bringing together contemporary technologies with ancient theatrical traditions. Our stories are rooted by an in-depth research process, drawing upon collaborations with leading experts in fields as diverse as histopathology, neuroscience and social science.

The company is led by Artistic Directors Liam Jarvis and Hannah Barker and Producer Ric Watts. Our associates and collaborators are drawn from a range of disciplines across writing, puppetry, devising and computer game design.

Our debut show *Mile End* premiered at the Edinburgh Fringe in 2007 to critical acclaim, picking up two awards (Fringe First, Arches Brick Award) and a further five nominations at the festival. The show has since toured the UK twice during 2008 and gave the company our international debut at the Pazz08 Festival in Germany.

Our second show *Beachy Head* premiered in the South East during 2009, prior to a successful run at the Edinburgh Festival, in co-production with New Wolsey Theatre, and a UK and International tour in 2011. The script has been published by Oberon Books.

In 2010 we created micro-performance *Lecture Notes on a Death Scene*, an immersive experience for single audience members, which was developed at the Pulse Fringe Festival, Farnham Maltings and The Lowry. It has since been seen at festivals around the UK.

That same year, we were also awarded a prestigious Theatre Sandbox commission to develop our interactive autobiographical performance event *Living Film Set*, in collaboration with The Junction and the Microsoft Research Labs, Cambridge.

2401 Objects is our new show and our first international co-production. The show premieres at the Edinburgh Festival in August 2011, and tours the UK in 2012.

'Meet the bright young things of British theatre' **Observer**

'Analogue is a young company certain to make its mark on British theatre' **The Guardian**

Analogue is an associate company of **Farnham Maltings**.
Analogue is a **National Theatre Studio** affiliate company.

www.analogueproductions.co.uk

THE NEW WOLSEY THEATRE

New Wolsey Theatre, Ipswich is a UK regional theatre with a national reputation for the quality, range and reach of its work and for embracing cultural diversity in the widest sense. The theatre is central to the creative life of Suffolk and seeks to expand the horizons of audiences and artists by presenting a programme designed to entertain, enrich and challenge.

The development of new talent is a priority for the New Wolsey and the annual PULSE Fringe Festival is a springboard for fresh new artistic voices, as well as a home for risk-taking and cutting-edge performance from more established artists. PULSE provides a platform for the development and presentation of new work by regional, British and international artists of vision, nurturing artistic ambition and excellence across a range of art forms including theatre, dance, comedy, music, event led visual arts, participatory theatre, physical theatre and circus led work.

For The New Wolsey Theatre
Chief Executive Sarah Holmes
Artistic Director Peter Rowe
Associate Director Rob Salmon
Technical Manager David Sherman

OLDENBURGISCHES STAATSTHEATER

Oldenburgisches Staatstheater is a repertory theatre in Oldenburg, Germany, with an extensive programme of opera, dance, theatre and children and youth theatre. The organisation produces both classic plays and operas, alongside a large programme of new writing, dance and devised theatre. The Staatstheater has recently undertaken a number of international co-productions with companies in Canada, Great Britain, Belgium and the Netherlands. Every two years the theatre organises a performing arts festival called PAZZ, which has recently programmed companies such as Third Angel, Rimini Protokoll and Theatre Replacement; and an international dance festival.

For Oldenburgisches Staatstheater
Artistic Director Markus Müller
Administration Director Tilmann Pröllochs
Dramaturg Jörg Vorhaben
PAZZ Festival Director Thomas Kraus

Hannah Barker is Co-Artistic Director and Co-founder of Analogue and also works as a journalist and education facilitator. She spent a year working in Tanzania before studying an undergraduate theatre degree at Royal Holloway, University of London, and then an MA in Advanced Theatre Practice at Central School of Speech and Drama. She further trained at The Desmond Jones School of Mime & Physical Theatre and The Actor's Studio. Hannah has written, directed and performed at the Edinburgh and Dublin Fringe festivals, the Pulse Festival and in London at the Battersea Arts Centre, the National Theatre Studio, the Pleasance, Hoxton Hall, The Young Vic and Hackney Empire. She has toured work and run workshops at regional venues nationwide and worked with companies abroad in the US, Africa and Europe. Hannah is a qualified journalist, having trained for her NCTJ in London and a certificate in Feature Writing at New York University. She currently writes for *YoungMinds Magazine*, politics.co.uk, Adfero news agency, *UK/US Review* and for international development charities including Sponsored Arts for Education (S.A.F.E.) which uses arts to educate on HIV/AIDS in Africa.

Alexander Fleischer is a Lighting Designer for theatre, concerts and exhibitions. Since 2007, he has been Lighting Designer at the Oldenburgisches Staatstheater for numerous opera (*Il Guistino*), theatre (*Baal, Die Räuber, Lisas Liebe*, etc.) and dance (*Motus*) productions. Further to his collaboration with Analogue, he has recently worked with Mammalian Diving Reflex, Toronto.

Alexander Garfath is a freelance creative sound designer and composer based in London. He has designed for over 30 productions in over 50 theatres across the UK and Europe since graduating from Central School of Speech and Drama with an MA in Sound Design and Music for Performance. He is the co-founder of performance collective Handheld Arts who are premiering their production *Paper Tom* at the Edinburgh Fringe this year. This production looks at Post Traumatic Stress Disorder in soldiers returning home from conflict and will be performed at Hill Street Theatre as part of ReMarkable Arts' 2011 programme. Previous work for Analogue includes *Mile End, Beachy Head,* and *Lecture Notes on a Death Scene*. Other previous credits include *Labour Exchange* (South Street, Reading), *Suffocation* (Oval House), *Bitch From Brixton, You Don't Kiss, The Laundry, Agamemnon* (Brockley Jack), *Naked Soldiers, A Fistful of Barton* (Warehouse Theatre, Croydon), *Progress* (Union), *Carbon Footprint Detective Agency* (LIFT/Arcola/London Tour), *5 Borough Youth Festival* (Stratford Circus), *Liz & Di* (London College of Fashion/Cochrane), *Transitions* (Bialystok Puppet Theatre, Poland/International Puppet Buskers Festival, Ghent, Belgium).

Melody Grove trained at RSAMD graduating in 2009 with the James Bridie Gold Medal for Acting. Previous theatre includes Gwendolen in *The Importance of Being Earnest* at The Lyceum (commended for the Ian Charleson Award 2010), Baroness Fantasia De Wharff in *Snow White and the Seven De Wharffs* at Macrobert Stirling, one-woman show *Room*, Chiziko in *One Thousand Paper Cranes*, W in *One Night Stand* at The Tron and Joanna in *The Girls of Slender Means* at the Assembly Rooms. Short film includes *A Stately Suicide* and *Sisters*. Radio plays include *A Case for Paul Temple*, *Of Mice and Men*, *The Vanishing*, *Philip and Sydney*, *The House of Mercy*, *La Princesse De Cleves* and numerous short stories for BBC Radio 4.

Thor Hayton is the Director and Founder of VI Created Media Ltd, with 16 years experience in computer aided design covering 3D modelling, multimedia, animation and visual effects. He has worked for companies such as Disney, Sony, Realtime Worlds and Climax, creating titles such as *Crackdown*, *Theme Park Inc*, *Split Second*, *Robot Wars*, *Sudeki*, *San Francisco Rush* and *Tron*. Thor has also worked as a Visiting Lecturer at Portsmouth University where he has done lectures on animation and teachings in Adobe After Effects, Max and Maya, created effects for the feature film *Travellers* and has worked for Milton Morrissey creating multimedia for the play *Buddy – The Buddy Holly Story*. Thor has been working with Analogue since it was formed in 2007 and was responsible for the Multimedia in *Mile End*, *Beachy Head*.

Lewis Hetherington is an associate artist of Analogue having co-written and performed in their first two shows: *Mile End* and *Beachy Head*, and most recently co-wrote *2401 Objects*. He is an associate artist with Imaginate, which has afforded him the chance to undertake research with Sense Scotland, exploring the creative possibilities of making theatre with and for young deaf blind adults. Lewis has lots of experience making theatre for and with young people, through working with companies including Starcatchers, Visible Fictions, RSAMD Dramaworks, Traverse and National Theatre of Scotland. Other writing credits include *bodies unfinished* (Grey Swan at the Brockley Jack), *Sea Change* and *A Perfect Child* for A Play, A Pie and A Pint at the Oran Mor, and adapting two Argentinian plays – *Instructions for Butterfly Collectors* and *The Archivist* – for the National Theatre of Scotland. Lewis made a show for young people; *Cloud Man* with Puppeteer Ailie Cohen, which is part of the 2011 Made In Scotland showcase at the Edinburgh Fringe Festival.

Liam Jarvis is Co-Director of Analogue. He graduated from the directing course at LAMDA in 2003, and subsequently worked with artists and institutions such as Gecko, Theatre-Rites, Chris Goode and The Young Vic. He co-founded Analogue, with whom he has been creating award-winning work since 2007, touring both the UK and internationally. Parallel to his work with Analogue, Liam completed an MA in Theatre Research in 2009 (with Distinction) and was subsequently offered an AHRC award to study as a Part-time PhD candidate at Royal Holloway University, researching interactive modes of live performance and contemporary sculpture, drawing on neuroscience. Liam is a Visiting Lecturer at Royal Holloway University, where he has taught contemporary theatre practices, devising and directing methodologies since 2004. He has run workshops and Master classes (both with Analogue and as a freelance practitioner at NT Discover, amongst other organisations) with both young students and experienced adults throughout the UK and abroad.

Pieter Lawman trained at the Royal Academy of Dramatic Art. Theatre work includes: *War Horse, The Revenger's Tragedy* (Royal National Theatre); *Macbeth, Much Ado About Nothing* (Shakespeare's Globe); *Tristan and Yseult, Rapunzel, A Matter Of Life And Death* (Kneehigh); *Swallows and Amazons* (Bristol Old Vic); *The Count of Monte Cristo* (West Yorkshire Playhouse); *Romeo and Juliet* (Ludlow Festival); *A Doll's House* (Exeter Northcott); *The Car Cemetery* (Gate Theatre); *Reverence* (Goat and Monkey); *Jason and the Argonauts* (Schtanhaus); *Release the Beat* (Arcola); *The Canterville Ghost, The Three Musketeers, Tartuffe, Head On* (Haymarket Theatre, Basingstoke). Television work includes: *The Inspector Lynley Mysteries; Lewis; Lennon Naked.* Radio work: *OK Computer*

Sebastien Lawson read drama at Hull University and the University of Washington, Seattle. As an award-winning theatre-maker and performer he has worked with numerous companies including Chris Goode's Signal to Noise (*Escapology / Homemade*), Plymouth Theatre Royal (*Speed Death of the Radiant Child*), the Royal Court Theatre (*First Time, First Love / Heart in Case*), Tangled Feet (*Home*), CPT (*Icarus 2.0*), Song Theatre (*Irreversible*), Sourfeast (*The Translator*), Metis Arts (*3rd Ring Out*), Unlimited Theatre (*Mission To Mars*) and Top of the World. He is co-founder of The Frequency D'ici, with whom he has created *Paperweight* and *Free Time Radical*, which premieres at Edinburgh Festival 2011. Alongside his devising work he has also worked as an actor in numerous roles in Theatre, TV and film.

Helen Mugridge is an experienced stage and production manager. Her previous credits include: *Total Football*, Ridiculusmus (Barbican Pit), *Beachy Head*, Analogue (National Tour and Switzerland), *Poetry for Morons*, Arlette George (Edinburgh Fringe 2010), *Everything Must Go*, Kristin Fredrickson (National Tour), *The Poof Downstairs*, Jon Haynes (National Tour), *Shoot/Get Treasure/Repeat* and *Eshara*, Cheekish Productions (National Tour), *Special*, fecund theatre (Edinburgh Festival 2007), *The Gruffalo*, Tall Stories (Soho Theatre and Canada Tour), *Hello You*, fecund theatre (Riverside Studios), *Say Nothing* and *Ideas Men*, Ridiculusmus (Barbican Pit), *Jungle* (BAC) and *Don Q* (Edinburgh Festival), Labyrinth Theatre. She also produces the work of the critically acclaimed fecund theatre and is on the board of Labyrinth Theatre for which she is also creative producer.

Anike Sedello studied Stage Design at The Academy of Fine Arts in Vienna and graduated with honours in 2006. While studying, she spent a semester abroad at the Wimbledon School of Art in London, studying Theatre Design. Since 2005 she has worked as a theatre designer for various scenic projects including *Wir alle für immer zusammen*, *Adams Äpfel*, *Nur ein Tag*, *Lisa's Liebe* (all Staatstheater Oldenburg), *39 Stufen* (Theater Wihelmshaven), *Spiel's noch mal Sam* (Stadttheater Pforzheim) and *Von Mücken, Elefanten und der Macht in den Händen* (Theater Bonn). *2401 Objects* is her first collaboration with Analogue.

Jörg Vorhaben studied Theatre Science and Sociologies at the Friedrich Alexander University Erlangen, Humboldt University Berlin and at the University of Amsterdam. During his studies he was an Assistant Director at the Maxim Gorki Theatre Berlin and worked for the ARENA Festival in Erlangen. He also worked with UK company Metro-Bolout-Dodo. He was previously dramaturg assistant at the Schauspiel Hannover. From 2000 to 2002 he was dramaturg at the Nationaltheater Mannheim and from 2002 till 2006 at the Schauspiel Köln. Since 2006, Jörg has been lead theatre dramaturg at the Oldenburgisches Staatstheater, where he is the artistic leader of the Go West Festival (Theatre from Belgium and the Netherlands) and curator for the PAZZ Festival. He is also board member of the Dramatugische Gesellschaft (DG) of Germany.

Ric Watts is an independent producer based in Manchester. Ric is Producer for Analogue, for whom he has produced *Mile End*, *Beachy Head*, *Lecture Notes on a Death Scene* and *Living Film Set*. Ric started his career at Your Imagination, where he produced work by Cartoon de Salvo, Ridiculusmus and Kazuko Hohki. Since 2006, Ric has produced a number of acclaimed touring productions, including: *FOOD* for theimaginarybody, *Particularly in the Heartland* by The TEAM, *The Adventures of Wound Man and Shirley* by Chris Goode, *Twelfth Night* by Filter and Schtanhaus, *Paperweight* by The Frequency D'ici, *Mission To Mars* by Unlimited Theatre, and *Running on Air* by Laura Mugridge. In 2010, Ric was Festival Producer for the 2010 Queer Up North International Festival, commissioning and programming a range of international artists over a two-week festival in Manchester. Ric is currently also Producer for Chris Goode & Company, The Frequency D'ici and Unlimited Theatre, and is developing projects with Royal & Derngate and The Other Way Works.

Directors' Notes

On 2 December 2009, a ground-breaking procedure took place live on the internet to a global audience of around 400,000 people; as the world looked on, Dr. Jacopo Annese and his team at The Brain Observatory, San Diego (University of California) sliced a human brain into thousands of histological sections. I was one of those 400,000 spectators, and this is where our relationship with Henry's story began.

In life, the brain belonged to Henry Gustav Molaison (1926-2008), more famously known as 'Patient HM'. Amongst the scientific community, HM and the research surrounding his condition are rigorously documented in over 11,900 published scientific journals. Meanwhile if you were to conduct a quick Google search for 'Patient HM' you would discover that the search produces in excess of 33 million results; he is one of the most written about amnesic case-studies in the history of neuroscience.

Since a young age, Henry had suffered from partial epileptic seizures, largely attributed to a bicycle accident he had had at the age of nine. Following his sixteenth birthday, Henry's illness became progressively further debilitating, suffering with several tonic-clonic seizures. By the time he reached his twenties he was living at home with his parents, with little or no social life, barely able to hold down a job at the local garage and taking maximum dosages of several prescribed anticonvulsants, none of which worked. In 1953, Henry and his parents resorted to drastic measures in an attempt to improve his quality of life; on August 25 1953, Henry underwent experimental brain surgery to contain the intractable seizures. Neurosurgeon, Dr. William Beecher Scoville (1906-1984) removed approximately two-thirds of his hippocampus, parahippocampal gyrus, and amygdala. The intervention brought some relief from the convulsions, but these benefits were greatly outweighed by an unforeseen and irreversible side effect. Soon after the operation, it became clear that Henry could no longer recognise hospital staff, he could not remember having solved the crossword puzzle he had just completed and entire events leading up to the time of the operation had vanished.

Henry was left with retrograde amnesia, and could not remember most events in the two-year period prior to the surgery. But perhaps even more disconcerting was the fact that Henry was also left with severe anterograde amnesia; a loss of the ability to create any new memories.

For all that has been written about him, since we initiated this research project our relationship with Henry has remained illusively virtual; but the idea of him has been a tangible presence in our rehearsal room over the two years this project has been developing. The extensive documentation that already exists made it apparent to us that what we did not want to make was a documentary piece about HM – given the readily available materials this would make the process feel reiterative; our aim was rather to consider the question of what could the experience of a theatre piece offer to the telling of this story?

Formally, theatre is perhaps more reliant on the hippocampus within the brains of its audience than any other medium, since memory is the only place where theatre truly lives beyond the immediate circumstance of the performance. Therefore, it is perhaps the form that best articulates the value of our own hippocampus; after all, what would the experience of a theatre performance mean for an audience of anterograde amnesics (knowing that within minutes of the curtain call the experience would have ceased to exist for that audience)?

It is through theatre and its unique properties that we understood the true gravity of Henry's loss, and found an affinity with Dr. Jacopo Annese in his desire for face-to-face encounters; for us the key encounter is with the audience during the performance event. For Jacopo, the most significant encounters are with his patients; the opportunity to meet them in life before carrying out such procedures in death represents a radical shift away from viewing patients as anonymous specimens, and rather seeks to connect the organs with the complex stories and human beings behind them. Dr. Jacopo uses science to help tell the story of a subject and their body, we use the theatre, with the belief that these different disciplines can usefully speak to one another.

Liam Jarvis

'What would you lose if you lost the last two years of your life?'

It was during rehearsals in October 2010 when the question was posed. The room was heavy with the weight of the subject we were tackling and, in that way that happens in a devising room, we had exploded out ideas to an intimidating scale.

The question silenced everyone as they scanned the last two years to assess their potential losses.

The entire creation of a piece of work, the birth of a child, two or three relationships, all vanished. A couple of influential interactions, a few flashes of pleasure and moments of pain, some seemingly inconsequential details that changed someone's mind or enforced an opinion, all disappeared.

The question referred to the two years that were wiped from Henry Molaison's memory preceding his operation in 1953. But, in fact, it also applied to the 55 years that followed it, until his death in December 2008.

Of course the question is flawed. For people in Henry's orbit, the world continued to turn during those years, and those who played supporting cast to his story had stories of their own which did not disappear.

And yet what is a relationship that is only remembered by one person? What losses do loved ones suffer by being partly or completely erased from the minds of those they care about?

By imagining the loss of my own history, I began to see beyond the countless medical journals, the phenomenal headlines and extraordinary science surrounding 'Patient HM' that had come to define Henry's story.

What emerged in their place was the human being at the centre. How a simple thing like turning short-term into long-term memory not only allows us to keep hold of precious moments and people and experiences that make up who we are, but also what we want to be. And how, without it, we are nowhere and we are incredibly vulnerable.

We found very few records of Henry's life before 1953. Consequently, we can only guess the events that led to Henry agreeing to undergo that fateful surgery, which even the surgeon who performed it described as 'frankly experimental'. We don't even know whether he or his family were fully aware of the level of risk involved in the procedure and who made the final decision.

Regardless, the choice they made led to an extraordinary situation, and meant others were responsible for deciding what was best for Henry for the rest of his life.

So what does it mean to decide something for someone's 'own

good'? How do we determine what is right for an individual in relation to what is best for the greater good? Can our motivations be separated from a seemingly innate human instinct to progress? We tend to plot our successes by our advances – in business terms: If you're not moving forwards, you're moving backwards. So where does that leave Henry?

Henry's story provokes a vast entanglement of ethical dilemmas, which we have attempted to engage with by creating a fictional story of Henry's life leading up to the procedure.

Throughout our process, we have sought extensive advice from neuroethics experts who have said that while good practice guides boast clear technical answers, in reality this is undeniably a messy area, especially with patients whose mental capacity is compromised.

Henry was visited by close to 100 scientists during his lifetime. His guardians signed waivers to allow them to run their experiments and while he appeared to happily consent, for him each one appeared as an isolated request. Was he even aware of what he was consenting to?

By presenting in the show the voice of the neuroscientist responsible for cutting Henry's brain into 2401 objects, it is not our aim to say we agree or disagree with his work or the work of the countless scientists conducting tests on Henry – after all, who are we to enforce our opinion when we are equally complicit in using Henry for our own gain?

But in staging this story and in offering the voice of one such neuroscientist, we hope *2401 Objects* will open a discussion that both addresses this subject's complexity, and also tells Henry's story not as 'the most famous neuroscientific brain of all time', to which he is mostly referred in the numerous case studies, but as a human being with aspirations, desires and potential he was tragically never able to enjoy.

Hannah Barker

Analogue

2401 OBJECTS

Written by Hannah Barker,
Lewis Hetherington & Liam Jarvis
Devised by the Company

Additional text drawn from transcripts
of telephone interviews with Dr Jacopo Annese

OBERON BOOKS
LONDON

First published in 2011 by Oberon Books Ltd
521 Caledonian Road, London N7 9RH
Tel: 020 7607 3637 / Fax: 020 7607 3629
e-mail: info@oberonbooks.com
www.oberonbooks.com

A catalogue record for this book is available from the British
Library.

ISBN: 978-1-84943-195-8

Cover Photography: Andreas J. Etter
Graphic Design: Liam Jarvis

Printed in Great Britain by CPI Antony Rowe, Chippenham.

Characters

1953: Hartford, Connecticut.

HENRY MOLAISON

MOTHER

FATHER

LAUREN

1988 – 2008: Bickford Health Centre, Connecticut.

PATIENT HM

NURSE

2011: The Brain Observatory, San Diego.

DR JACOPO ANNESE

A Word on the Set

The set for the original production of *2401 Objects* centred on a large piece of scenic equipment we called the 'Macrotome'.

Its design was inspired by the cryomicrotome which was used to dissect Henry Molaison's brain; the blade cuts once across the brain to remove a micro thin slice, and then resets to its original point ready to repeat the same process.

The 'Macrotome' consisted of a large steel frame inside which was a gauze projection screen. The construction could glide upstage and downstage on tracks, operated by the Stage Manager and actors. There was an aperture underneath the structure so as it travelled downstage towards a scene, objects and performers could disappear underneath it – when it was then pulled back upstage, the space would be clear.

Actors could perform in front of the screen or behind it, so they would appear inside the projected image. The screen could also revolve within its frame, allowing larger items of set – tables, standard lamps – to come on and off.

The screen could also revolve within its frame, allowing larger items of set – tables, standard lamps – to come on and off.

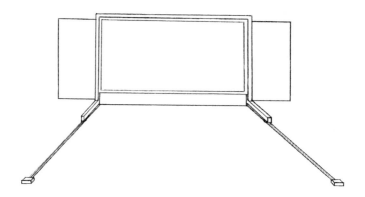

The stage is empty except for a microphone on a stand to one side. A recording made at the Brain Observatory in San Diego of DR JACOPO ANNESE is heard:

Ladies and Gentlemen. Hello, this is Dr Annese from San Diego.

I have been asked to say what do I do for a job and it is not a very easy answer at the moment because I thought I was an anatomist, and I think I became more of a storyteller, and I tell stories about patients who have something wrong with their brains.

And lately I've been telling stories about people who have nothing wrong with their brains but who wish to donate their brains to science and... I think I've confused you enough.

Well I apologise for not being there and, nonetheless I am making this recording for Analogue. And I was asked to welcome you the audience on account of the work I have done with Henry Molaison.

Now Henry is the reason why everyone is here. The performers, the audience, and my voice too, We're all here because of him. Because of what he did in his life. Because of what happened to him. Because of what they did to him. Me included.

And I would like to be there and speaking in person but I can't, so somebody is actually gonna speak on my behalf. I haven't met him but I trust that he will do a very good job.

The company enter stage with furniture to set up Bickford Health Centre. One actor takes their place at the microphone and puts on a jacket to play DR JACOPO ANNESE. The jacket is worn every time the actor plays this role during the show.

And I think now it's time for me to leave the stage to the real actors.

DR JACOPO ANNESE: Ladies and Gentlemen. Hello. For the next hour, I am Doctor Annese.

We decided it was important that I was here in some way and could tell you face to face something of the stories I have played a part in, like that of Henry Molaison.

A performer takes his place as HM, sitting on his chair at the Bickford Health Centre.

One of the most important brains in the world.

But I've been asked to just tell you about a flight I made. It was February 2009 and I remember I was sat on this plane, very normal plane, wings, aisles, overhead lockers. We were getting ready for take off. And as the engines were growling into life and we started along the runway, I was excited because it was a momentous flight really. Momentous – for me – because of the reason I was travelling.

And the reason was Henry.

A rush of sound as plane takes off.

2.

A NURSE is walking through a projected corridor of Bickford Care Centre. As she reaches the end she turns, we see her in a window waving at HM from the corridor.

HM sits alone in his room, as the light of the TV flickers on his face. Extracts from the film 'To Have and Have Not' are heard:

Extract 1:

FEMALE VOICE: *I'm not gonna let you do it.*

MALE VOICE: *Why not? He's no different from anyone else just a little sicker that's all. It means he's not worth so much now let me – You can have another crack at me later on.*

Extract 2:

FEMALE VOICE: *Anybody got a match?*

Sound of box of matches being thrown and a match being lit.

Thanks.

At the end of the corridor the NURSE turns and enters HM's room. He is 65. HM treats her as if he's not met her before: friendly but unsure. She has worked with him for a year.

HM: Hello.

NURSE: Hi Henry, how are you today?

HM: Very well thank you.

NURSE: Beautiful day.

HM: Yes.

NURSE: Do you want some breakfast?

HM: Orange juice and hot buttered toast please.

Train rushes by outside the window.

Oh, there goes a train.

NURSE: Yes, I wonder where it's going.

I brought the crossword.

HM: I'll tell you who likes a crossword. My Father.

NURSE: Did you ever do them together?

HM: Oh no. He would do them on his own before dinner. I can see him there. With a Bourbon. He would take a sip when he didn't know an answer.

NURSE: Really?

HM: Oh yes. I can see it very clearly. At the dinner table. Mother cooking something lovely in the kitchen. My Father at his end of the table doing the crossword.

NURSE: I have a crossword here for you Henry.

HM: Well how funny!

NURSE: Would you like it?

HM: Yes please!

NURSE: What does that first one say?

HM: 19th Century Russian novelist, Seven Letters.

Pause.

Tolstoy.

NURSE: I can never get the answers to these things. How do you do it?

HM: I don't know. Do you have a pen?

NURSE: No. I'll get you one.

NURSE turns to leave, puts her hand in her pocket, turns back to him.

Oh no I've got one here.

NURSE offers him the pen.

HM: What?

NURSE: A pen for your crossword.

HM takes a moment to process the situation.

HM: Right.

NURSE: I'll get your breakfast.

HM: Hot buttered toast please.

NURSE: Great.

NURSE exits. HM is alone.

HM: 19th Century Russian novelist.

Pause, and then it comes to him, as if for the first time.

Tolstoy.

The Macrotome moves forward and clears the stage.

3.

Hartford, Connecticut, 1953. HENRY is mowing the lawn. It is a beautiful day. LAUREN appears in the garden next door. She almost glows in the sunlight.

On the projection screen, a white picket fence appears against a brilliant blue sky.

'Don't Let The Stars Get In Your Eyes' by Perry Como plays over transition and then crossfades as if heard coming from an open window.

LAUREN: Hello.

　　HENRY can't hear her.

　　He switches the lawnmower off.

LAUREN: Hello.

HENRY: Hello.

LAUREN: Beautiful day.

HENRY: That's exactly what I was about to say.

LAUREN: The sun is –

HENRY: Yes. I interrupted. Sorry.

LAUREN: It's ok –

HENRY: But I was going to say that the sun gets people out the house. It's nice.

LAUREN: Yes.

HENRY: You're reading.

LAUREN: I am.

HENRY: What is it?

LAUREN: Oh some thing. It's science fiction. It's meant to be very good.

HENRY: Is it?

LAUREN: No. It's…It's rather boring. People flying about in spaceships, talking to each other with their minds. There was nothing else. This one bit, a woman gets excited because of a special type of futuristic fridge! Can you imagine? Hundreds of years in the future, and all this woman can get excited about, is a fridge.

HENRY: I think my mother would get excited about a fridge from the future.

LAUREN: Maybe I should give this to her?

HENRY: Oh we've got lots of books.

LAUREN: Really?

HENRY: My mother reads. A lot.

LAUREN: Do you?

HENRY: Not really. But I could have a look for you if –

LAUREN: That would be great.

HENRY: Great.

LAUREN: What's your name?

HENRY: Henry.

LAUREN: Henry. Good name. I had a dog called Henry.

HENRY: Was he a nice dog?

LAUREN: Very nice.

HENRY: What's your name?

LAUREN: Lauren.

HENRY: I've never had a dog called Lauren. Not that that's… Are you back from college?

LAUREN: Yes. Just back for the summer. It's nice to be away. People at college are stupid.

HENRY: That's not what you expect.

LAUREN: No. You're back for the summer too?

HENRY: Yes. Sort of. No. I live here. With my parents.

LAUREN: All the time?

HENRY: Yes.

Pause.

HENRY: I've not been well…

LAUREN: Sorry. But you're getting better?

HENRY: I'm. It's…

Pause.

LAUREN: You're doing a good job with the lawn.

HENRY: Thanks.

LAUREN: Sorry I shouldn't have asked about, forget I said…
The sun's shining, it's a beautiful day. That's all there is to
think about.

HENRY: Yes.

LAUREN: Oh, and the book, actually. You should think about
finding me a book.

HENRY: Yes. Of course. What would you, maybe something
with adventure or…

LAUREN: No. Well maybe something epic, but romantic and
old –

HENRY: Historical.

LAUREN: Yes.

HENRY: From the past, not the –

LAUREN: Exactly. Oh and. But then you might not have
anything like –

HENRY: We have lots of books.

LAUREN: Maybe something French. Or Russian.

A call from offstage 'Lauren!'

LAUREN: That's my Father.

HENRY: Russian?

LAUREN: But in English.

HENRY: Yes.

The same voice calls again 'Lauren!'

LAUREN: I've got to go in, lovely to meet you Henry. See you soon.

HENRY: Yes. Yeah. Bye. Yes.

4.

'Look At That Girl' by Guy Mitchell plays during transition.

The family dining room appears with a table emerging through a revolving screen – a projection of a modest chandelier and wallpaper appears in the background.

HENRY has a drink for his FATHER and some water for himself. Throughout this scene the dialogue often overlaps and runs on quickly. HENRY opens a bottle and takes a pill.

FATHER: Is that? Do you take one of those ones in the evening as well?

HENRY: Yes. The Doctor changed it.

FATHER: Quite a few isn't there?

HENRY nods.

FATHER: Righto. Good man.

HENRY: Trouble with the crossword?

FATHER: No. Just need one more, just…

HENRY: You never get the last –

FATHER: I will I will.

MOTHER enters, looks over the FATHER's shoulder

MOTHER: Wombat.

FATHER: Darling that's… Thank you.

MOTHER: It was an easy one. Dinner's going to be in fifteen minutes. I hope you're hungry.

HENRY: Starving.

MOTHER: Really?

HENRY: I was outside all day.

FATHER: Lucky you.

MOTHER: How was the office darling?

FATHER: Sweltering.

HENRY: The garden was lovely, nice breeze.

FATHER: You were meant to be working!

HENRY: I was.

FATHER: I'm teasing. Lawn is impeccable.

HENRY: Thank you. I took my time. Spoke to the neighbours over the fence.

FATHER: Number twenty three? That's Mrs Rumsden is it?

MOTHER: Yes.

FATHER: She has a very annoying voice doesn't she?

HENRY: No.

MOTHER: She does Henry she's like a banshee.

FATHER: Why were you talking to her?

HENRY: No, over the other fence. Nineteen.

MOTHER: The Olsons?

HENRY: Their daughter.

FATHER: Oh.

MOTHER: Oh.

   That sounds –

FATHER: Yes I've seen her, pretty isn't she?

MOTHER: Now –

FATHER: What? She is.

HENRY: I didn't notice.

FATHER: You can spot a pretty girl Henry –

HENRY: Well –

FATHER: – or what are those spectacles for?

HENRY: We were just talking!

MOTHER: Of course. That's lovely.

FATHER: What were you talking about?

HENRY: Books.

FATHER: She's a reader. Like your mother.

HENRY: Yes. But no.

FATHER: Clever. That's all right these days, a clever woman.

HENRY: She was nice.

FATHER: Was she?

HENRY: Stop it.

MOTHER: What was she reading?

HENRY: Something about spaceships, and telepathy –

MOTHER: She's reading science fiction?

HENRY: She doesn't like it.

MOTHER: Good.

HENRY: I thought about. Well we have a lot of books.

MOTHER: We do.

HENRY: So I thought I could have a look and –

FATHER: And lend her a book.

MOTHER: Oh lovely.

FATHER: Your mother needs more space –

MOTHER: I do.

FATHER: – do her good to get rid of some –

MOTHER: Mm hmm.

HENRY: Well –

FATHER: – give a whole series of books.

HENRY: Oh yes! Piles of books!

FATHER: Where would you start?

HENRY: No I er –

FATHER: Just for fun, what would you choose?

HENRY: I don't know about books. She knows what she likes, she said –

MOTHER: What?

HENRY: She said she likes romantic books –

FATHER: Romance!

HENRY: – historical, she also said historical.

FATHER: She wants you to romance her!

HENRY: No! Stop it!

MOTHER: 'Gone With The Wind'

HENRY: That's American isn't it?

FATHER: Why?

HENRY: She said French. I think she'd like to travel.

FATHER: You did talk a lot.

HENRY: I just got the impression.

FATHER: Very forward.

MOTHER: She sounds wonderful.

HENRY: She's nice.

FATHER: Well that's it. You can woo her with romantic French novels –

HENRY: She said Russian too.

FATHER: Did she? She's not…

MOTHER: Of course not.

FATHER: No. No. But a little book, possibly French, a little note in the front cover, a poem.

HENRY: A poem?

FATHER: She likes words.

MOTHER: Press a flower in between the pages.

FATHER: No, no, don't do that son, too much.

HENRY: Poems aren't too much?

FATHER: No. You want to make a gesture.

HENRY: Well maybe I should just take her to France?

FATHER: Yes! You can put the tickets, in the book.

MOTHER: You can go to Paris!

HENRY: Propose on top of the Eiffel Tower…

MOTHER: Yes!

FATHER: Get married…

MOTHER: Tour through Europe on your honeymoon.

HENRY: I'll send a postcard.

FATHER: You might be busy being romantic.

HENRY: Dad!

MOTHER: You're terrible.

FATHER: So, grandchildren.

HENRY: No –

MOTHER: Oh yes.

FATHER: A good few would be nice, four to five –

HENRY: Forty-five!

FATHER: Absolutely.

FATHER exits.

HENRY: They can all learn French –

MOTHER: You'll live in Montmartre with the artists. I'd love to go to Paris.

HENRY: Well you can come and visit my imaginary house out there.

MOTHER: Of course. Lovely. I'll book my tickets.

FATHER returns.

FATHER: Here we go.

HENRY: What's that?

FATHER: A book.

MOTHER: 'War and Peace'?

FATHER: I've not read it obviously. Russian, but look, the first bit – in French.

MOTHER: There's lots of French bits in it. Napoleon even.

FATHER: Is it a history book?

MOTHER: No.

FATHER: What's Napoleon doing in it?

MOTHER: Well there's lots of real bits but lots of made up bits too. To make sense of it all.

FATHER: Ok ok so not a history book, but historical, and there is romance?

MOTHER: Oh yes.

HENRY: What do you want me to…?

FATHER: Take it over.

HENRY: But…

FATHER: Come on. Take it now. Knock on the door and say –

HENRY: No…

FATHER: – lovely to chat to you today and…

HENRY: I don't. No. It's late and –

FATHER: Where's this come from?

HENRY: – I might not be well enough –

FATHER: You're fine we were just talking about this, laughing and

HENRY: – it was silly.

FATHER: No you said you were going to lend her a book –

HENRY: I said I was going to have forty-five children I was –

FATHER: Don't be smart Henry you said you'd take the book.

MOTHER: Look I think –

HENRY: I never said I would –

MOTHER: It's all right let's –

FATHER: No. You had a nice chat to her you were fine, she's not enjoying her book –

MOTHER: Let's not make a fuss.

FATHER: You're making a fuss. Just take the book.

HENRY: I haven't had an episode all day and –

FATHER: Do it.

HENRY: No.

FATHER: Then I will. I'll say it's from you.

HENRY: Please no.

MOTHER: Give me the book.

FATHER: You're going to let her down. I'll leave it on the porch, write a note from you.

HENRY: No.

FATHER: Why not?

HENRY: Because I'm almost thirty and –

FATHER: And you're so grown up every night at home with your parents –

HENRY: I don't want to go over there and have a –

FATHER: Don't you –

HENRY: – if I'm talking to her and –

FATHER: We've been here ten minutes. You could have been there and back.

MOTHER: That's enough now.

HENRY: I don't want to go over and –

FATHER: I'm taking it

MOTHER: No.

HENRY: I don't want to go over there and have a seizure in front of her –

FATHER: Henry I won't listen to you –

HENRY: – to collapse and shaking and fitting and bite my tongue and piss myself at her feet and –

FATHER: No. No Henry. No. Fine. We'll do nothing. That's right. We'll sit here and do nothing as we always do. Sit here and do nothing and and just… Just quietly disappoint each other for the rest of our lives.

HENRY: I don't want to. I don't want to be a disappointment.

MOTHER: No. You aren't you…

HENRY: It's not my fault. I don't want to be –

FATHER: When's dinner ready?

MOTHER: Five minutes.

FATHER: Excellent.

FATHER exits, followed by MOTHER. The chandelier light flickers and the wallpaper peels off the walls – the screen rotates and the table is taken off. As the screen rotates HENRY can be seen pacing with anger, then as the screen turns again he is seen lying in bed.

5.

HENRY is alone in his bedroom, looking out his bedroom window.

His FATHER is heard from offstage.

FATHER: You coming back down Henry?

    Henry?

HENRY: Yeah I. I think I'm going to go to bed.

FATHER: Okay. Great job on the lawn. We could do the hedge together tomorrow.

HENRY: Mmm. Night.

FATHER: You can show me how it's done –

HENRY: Yeah. Good night.

FATHER: Good night Henry. Good night.

> *HENRY continues to look out the window. LAUREN appears. She is cinematically framed brushing her hair, looking out into the night, listening to 'Half A Photograph' by Kay Starr. She is unaware that HENRY is watching her.*
>
> *The Macrotome moves forward. There is a change in the room. The music fills the space. LAUREN appears and her arm wraps itself around HENRY's body. LAUREN folds her body around HENRY's. They are happy and comfortable.*
>
> *The Macrotome moves forward again. It moves back to reveal that LAUREN has disappeared. HENRY is alone.*

6.

HM sits alone with only the TV light flickering on his face. Lauren Bacall's song 'How Little We Know' from 'To Have and Have Not' is heard coming from the TV.

Lights come up as the music crossfades to background ambience and the nurse appears next to him and the scene begins.

NURSE: Really?

HM: What?

NURSE: You were saying, one time your Father spun your Mother around the room? It was something to do with this film?

HM: Ah yes.

NURSE: They just had a bit of a dance?

HM: The film made me think of it.

NURSE: You remember the film?

HM: Oh yes. Very well. You know how Lauren Bacall says 'Anybody got a match?'

NURSE: Mm hmm.

HM: You see one time my Mother couldn't get the stove to work so she said –

NURSE: Ah she said 'Anybody got a match?'

HM: And it made my Father think of the film.

NURSE: Of course.

HM: So he did his best Humphrey Bogart –

NURSE: Right.

HM: – swooped in like a real romantic lead.

NURSE: How nice.

HM: Yes exactly, and my Father took my Mother's hand, like this –

NURSE: Did he?

NURSE has to drop the towel to the floor to take his hand.

They dance getting carried away around the room.

HM: – and he spun her round the room.

NURSE: That's lovely.

HM: It was.

NURSE: Right. I'll get you your breakfast?

HM: Hot buttered toast please.

NURSE: Of course.

NURSE goes to exit and then remembers she has left the towel and goes back for it. HM sees her as she comes back into his line of sight, he greets her, forgetting he saw her only moments ago.

HM: Hello.

NURSE: Hello Henry. I'll get you your breakfast.

HM: Hot buttered toast please. And some orange juice.

NURSE: Of course.

As NURSE is about to exit again, the film reminds HM of the same moment of his parents dancing.

HM: Oh this is, this reminds me of when my Mother couldn't get the stove to work.

NURSE: Oh.

HM: She couldn't get the stove to light so she said –

NURSE: Ah she said 'Anybody got a match?'

HM: And it made my Father think of the film.

NURSE: Of course.

HM: So he did his best Humphrey Bogart –

NURSE: Right.

HM: – swooped in like a real romantic lead.

NURSE: How nice!

HM: Yes exactly, and my Father took my Mother's hand, like this –

NURSE: did he?

They dance.

HM: – and he spun her round the room.

NURSE: That's lovely. Now. I'll get you your breakfast.

7.

DR JACOPO ANNESE on-board an American Airlines flight from Boston to San Diego, 16 February 2009.

The same actor continues to play DR JACOPO ANNESE at the microphone while another actor plays JACOPO's hands on the projection via a live video feed.

DR JACOPO ANNESE: So we're up in the air now. The plane is, you know, cruising along nicely. And I'm just, a lot, with my own thoughts. I'm listening to music, Ennio Morricone if I remember rightly,

Ennio Morricone 'Once Upon a Time in the West' is heard as if through headphones. The projection comes up to reveal hands scrolling through music on an MP3 player, echoing what we see the actor at the microphone doing with another MP3 player as if the two pairs of hands are the same.

I'm thinking of HM, Henry. And that excitement is still there, but also, I'm a little anxious. I don't want to be the second person to get it wrong.

I'm talking of Dr Scoville, who did the surgery in 1953. He was, of course, attempting to cure Henry's epilepsy, but instead created the world's most famous amnesic. The thing is, Scoville was dedicated to advancing his craft, but at the same time, he did the operation with tools he bought from a hardware store. Which is something he was sort of, proud of.

Cutting through the skull to see the brain – the art of trepanation – has been around for centuries.

A window appears in the set. We see the hands on the projection in a small square of light.

But still, it takes a certain, confidence, to go into someone's head. Let alone with such simple tools.

Air Hostess appears with meal.

I was brought along a little, you know. My meal. A very friendly Air Hostess, and I remember, for some reason, the colour of her nail varnish. It's funny the things that get stored away. The moments your brain makes permanent.

I used to work as a chef, and we had a saying 'the first bite is with the eye' and I always think with airplane food, your eyes give you a good indication of what you're about to... endure.

But anyway, Doctor Scoville.

We see moments of coincidence between the eating of the food, and the description of the 1953 procedure on HENRY. These moments hint at the text but are not overtly illustrative.

First he had to pull down the skin from Henry's forehead. Then, he uses a hole saw – the type you wind by hand – to cut through the skull. Just above one of the eye sockets, he grinds through the bone and removes a disc of about three centimetres in diameter. He repeats this procedure above the other eye. Two holes. Now he can see the brain.

A grey gelatinous mass, behind the eyes, the frontal lobes, which he moves aside to see the innermost part of the brain. He is looking for the hippocampus, the hippocampii, buried right inside. Shaped like two little seahorses. No one in 1953 knew what the hippocampus was for - in fact there are still lots of questions now – but surgeons at the time were doing similar procedure on epileptics and having some success when half of it was removed. But Scoville decided to take out the whole thing.

He cut the tissue so as to detach the hippocampus from the rest of the brain, and then with a little metal tube, he sucked that little greyish pink mass out of Henry's head. Gone.

All in all, he takes out enough neuronal tissue to easily fill an espresso cup.

He snaps a few tiny metal clips onto the frayed lesion
to seal it and then does as good a job as he can putting
Henry's head back as it was.

The Air Hostess comes and takes the meal away.

It's easy now of course to go, 'woah', but he was... He
wanted to do something bold, but also to get into Henry's
head and fix things. He was that kind of guy, you know.
He drove fast cars! I guess what I'm saying is he was
flamboyant, boisterous even, and maybe that's what led
him to do the operation. We don't know I guess.

But we do know that in 1953 Dr William Beecher Scoville
removed the hippocampii from Henry Molaison's
brain and left us with this artefact – which sort of makes
archaeologists of us all – this artefact, Patient H.M.

8.

The Family dining room appears with HENRY and his FATHER. HENRY has a lot of medicine bottles which he is taking pills from. It is visible in HENRY that he is weak and drained.

FATHER: So that one is…?

HENRY: It's a new one. It's supposed to be very good.

FATHER: Right. Shouldn't your Mother help?

HENRY: I know what I'm doing.

FATHER: Ok. What's that one?

HENRY: It's to stop the, to stop me from having a…

FATHER: Yes. Right. And…

HENRY: These three are all supposed to do that too. But then this one gives me headaches so I take that one.

FATHER: Right.

MOTHER enters.

MOTHER: Anybody got a match?

HENRY: No, sorry.

FATHER: What was that?

MOTHER: Anybody got a match?

FATHER: You, you're… Say it again.

MOTHER: Anybody got a match?

FATHER: Say it properly. Like the film. Lauren Bacall.

MOTHER: Oh yes of course.

FATHER: Go on. Say it again.

MOTHER: Really?

FATHER: Go on just for fun, go on.

MOTHER reluctantly goes out.

FATHER: Watch and learn Henry.

MOTHER re-enters, takes up her Lauren Bacall pose, ready to recreate the moment from the film 'To Have and Have Not.

MOTHER: Anybody got a match?

FATHER, takes on Humphrey Bogart. He gets a box of matches from his pocket, and throws them to her. She catches them, strikes one and lights an imaginary cigarette. She throws them back.

MOTHER: Thanks.

They break the pretence and laugh, FATHER makes his way to MOTHER, offers his hand, he spins her around, they dance.

MOTHER: You're very romantic this evening!

FATHER: Well I am in the company of a movie star.

MOTHER: Not quite!

FATHER: You could be. Couldn't she Henry?

MOTHER: You're embarrassing him!

FATHER: No, your Mother could make it in Hollywood couldn't she?

HENRY: Yes. I think so.

MOTHER: Really?

HENRY: Yes, you'd be a big success.

MOTHER: Well I should go then.

HENRY: You should.

MOTHER: Just turn up in Hollywood and –

FATHER: You'll get spotted in the street.

HENRY: And make a big hit movie.

MOTHER: Wonderful, I'll get very rich –

FATHER: And buy us a big mansion in the Hills.

MOTHER: I want to do serious roles –

FATHER: Of course.

MOTHER: – and win an Oscar.

HENRY: There will be lots of parties to go to.

MOTHER: I'll need lots of dresses.

FATHER: Absolutely.

HENRY: We'll spend our days lying by the pool.

MOTHER: I could try a cocktail!

FATHER: The sunshine, the beaches, the restaurants.

MOTHER: Perfect.

FATHER: It would be wouldn't it? To actually do it. Just for a week. It would be perfect.

Pause.

HENRY: You could go away on holiday if you want.

MOTHER: No. No.

HENRY: But if you –

MOTHER: We were just playing the game.

FATHER: Yes.

HENRY: But a holiday might be nice.

MOTHER: Being here as a family is nice isn't it?

FATHER: Absolutely.

HENRY: I could ask Mrs Rumsden next door if she would –

MOTHER: Oh no I wouldn't have you –

HENRY: But she could look after me maybe.

MOTHER: I don't think so.

HENRY: I wouldn't be too much trouble.

MOTHER: It's not about that it's, it's…

FATHER: I'd never get the time off work.

MOTHER: No you wouldn't.

FATHER: I've told you about my boss Henry, fierce.

MOTHER: Mm hmm.

FATHER: You remember in February I had to work two weekends in a row? A week in Hollywood? No chance!

MOTHER: No way.

HENRY: I don't want you to not go on holiday because of me.

MOTHER: Well now, that is just, that is silly.

HENRY starts to gather up all the medicines from the table, he can't hold them all at once.

FATHER: Do you need a hand?

HENRY: I'm fine.

HENRY begins to exit, and drops the medicines on the floor.

FATHER: Are you alright?

HENRY: I'm fine. I'm just a little…

MOTHER: What is it? What's wrong?

HENRY: I'm just a little, dizzy. You don't need to panic every time I –

MOTHER: No of course not, sorry Henry.

HENRY exits.

MOTHER and FATHER are alone.

FATHER: I could get the time off work.

MOTHER: Darling, I know.

FATHER: Just a week. To unwind. But we can't.

MOTHER: No.

FATHER: And I mean, we couldn't, we couldn't leave him with Mrs Rumsden could we?

MOTHER: Look I understand. I do. I want to go away. Sometimes I feel if I don't get away I'll break, something inside will be pulled so tightly it will snap and I'll break, shut down. But I won't. We won't.

FATHER: No. We can't leave him.

MOTHER: He had nine episodes last Tuesday.

FATHER: Nine, in one day?

MOTHER: I think it was nine. It might have been eight. That day he didn't come down for dinner.

FATHER: You should have told me.

MOTHER: It's just. He's. Nine, eight, five, ten, what does it matter?

They both look at the table and the space where HENRY was standing.

FATHER: Do you think they're working, the drugs?

MOTHER: Dr Scoville said that it may be a while before they take effect.

FATHER: They have had an effect. He's sleeping more. Talking less.

MOTHER: He's nice.

FATHER: I'm not disputing that.

MOTHER: He does the garden.

FATHER: And how long do we keep pretending that is a miraculous achievement?

MOTHER: What are you saying?

FATHER: I'm saying don't you ever think about who he was supposed to be? Our son the engineer, the police officer. Our son who married the girl next door, and who are expecting their second, third child and they all live together in a big house, and he comes to visit and looks me in the eye and I know I have done a good job.

MOTHER: You can't live in make believe.

FATHER: I know. So we should talk to Dr Scoville again.

MOTHER: No. No one is getting inside Henry's head.

FATHER: I just mean to ask more about the procedure.

MOTHER: It involves cutting through his head and taking out bits of his brain. I'm not sure I want to know any more.

FATHER: No of course, I'm not saying we do it. No. I'm saying he is good at his job, he has had some success –

MOTHER: Yes with people in asylums. It's one thing to do these experiments on people who are broken in the head –

FATHER: Henry's broken in the head.

MOTHER: He's your son.

FATHER: Yes, yes, but…

MOTHER: You're not suggesting we take this surgery seriously?

FATHER: No. No. Of course not. It's a last resort. We would have to be, I don't know, at breaking point.

MOTHER: What do you mean?

FATHER: Look I realise I'm failing to keep this family together the way I should. Which is why I'm suggesting going back to Dr Scoville, to ask about other possible treatments. I don't mean the surgery. I just, if he had any other ideas.

MOTHER: I suppose we have to keep thinking of what we can do.

FATHER: Yes. What we might have to do.

HENRY enters.

HENRY: Hello.

MOTHER: Oh hello. You seem cheerful.

HENRY: I am. I'm feeling good.

FATHER: Are you going somewhere?

HENRY: I'm just going out for some fresh air. Just in the garden. Is that ok?

MOTHER: Of course. Go ahead. We'll be here.

HENRY exits.

Pause.

FATHER: Shall I go or…

MOTHER: It's all right I'll go.

MOTHER exits the same direction as HENRY.

9.

On the projection screen, a white picket fence appears against a brilliant blue sky.

HENRY and LAUREN in the garden, she is holding the book.

LAUREN: I thought you'd forgotten.

HENRY: It just took a while.

LAUREN: What were you doing? Writing it?

HENRY: Ha. No.

LAUREN: Really. Where have you been? Are you all right?

HENRY: Yep.

LAUREN: Did you get unwell again?

HENRY: No I'm fine.

LAUREN: It's all right if you aren't –

HENRY: Nope. I'm one hundred per cent. Is the book ok?

LAUREN: Perfect. What's it about?

HENRY: War. And…

LAUREN: And Peace. You've not read it then?

HENRY: No. But it is historical and romantic.

LAUREN: I feel bad taking it if you haven't –

HENRY: No but I thought, well, we have the summer –

LAUREN: Half the summer.

HENRY: Yes half but… Read it together. We could read it together. Take turns, doing chapters out loud.

LAUREN: Really?

HENRY: Yeah. Or just. Well.

LAUREN: That sounds nice.

HENRY: I could make iced tea, and you could read the first chapter.

LAUREN: Great.

HENRY: Great ok that sounds –

HENRY is broken off as he falls to the ground and has a violent seizure.

10.

HM is asleep in his chair in the health centre. LAUREN enters as if coming around into HENRY's garden. By the time she arrives HENRY has left the stage but the sound of his fit continues. LAUREN moves towards where HENRY was, then goes to sit next to HM. She hugs him, her head on his shoulder.

The scene plays as if a dream and the sound and light reflect this. HENRY appears at his bedroom window, which is projected on the screen, he looks out over the scene.

LAUREN: Henry are you awake?

11.

This scene overlaps the previous one and HM remains onstage.

HENRY is ill. He is in his bedroom, staring out of his window. HENRY's MOTHER is heard from the other side of the bedroom door.

'Outside Of Heaven' by Eddie Fisher, continues in the background of the scene.

MOTHER: Henry. It's a beautiful day.

    Why don't you come outside? I made some lemonade.

HENRY: I'm not… I'm not thirsty.

MOTHER: It's been… You've been in your room for days now, don't you, don't you want to –

HENRY: What?

MOTHER: – sit on the lawn. The Olsons are about, they're packing the car. Lauren's going back to college. You could –

HENRY: I want to stay here thank you.

LAUREN appears looking at HENRY in his window. A car engine starts. She has a brief exchange with HENRY.

They can't hear each other; LAUREN is heard as she is outside the house, though HENRY is not heard from behind the glass of his bedroom window.

LAUREN: I'm going back to college. Why don't you come down? I came round to see you, but you would never come down. I've got your book.

HENRY is really trying to reply in gesture and overly emphasised mouthing.

    I can't hear you.

A car engine starts.

    I've got to go.

There is a moment where HENRY is seen in his window, and HM goes to his window. They both look into the distance. HM watches a train go by.

HM: I wonder where she's going.

12.

HM is alone at the window. The TV light is flickering and then an extract from 'To Have and Have Not' is heard through the speakers.

FEMALE VOICE: *You're not to touch him d'ya hear?*

MALE VOICE: *Well that's alright with me I'm not getting paid.*

2ND MALE VOICE: *Please she does not know what she's saying she's not herself.*

The room lights up, the NURSE is there and the scene suddenly begins.

NURSE: I'm just saying I was calling, I didn't know if you were awake.

HM: Sorry.

NURSE: Don't worry about it. What are you up to?

HM: Not much.

NURSE: You up to mischief?

HM: Oh, just a little!

NURSE: Well I've got my eye on you. Horrible day isn't it? That rain.

HM: Like a cow pissing on a flat rock.

NURSE: Henry!

HM: You're like my mother, she got mad when I said that once.

NURSE: I'm not surprised, your poor mum.

HM: I think I was fourteen and we were at the dinner table and the rain was hammering down and I said that and she went so red I thought she was going to explode.

NURSE: Where did you learn it from?

HM: I remember it was what all the kids were saying. When you're at school you'll try anything to fit in.

NURSE: That's true. I've got the crossword here.

HM: Oh good I like a crossword.

NURSE: Great. I'll read the first one.

NURSE comes to help him over to his chair.

HM: Have you seen this rain?

NURSE: Oh yes. It's like a cow pissing on a flat rock.

HM: Ho! You're a lively one!

NURSE: I am indeed. Shall we sit you down?

HM: Why?

NURSE: I thought you might like to do the crossword.

HM moves supported by the NURSE towards the chair and picks up the remote control off it.

HM: What's this?

NURSE: A remote control.

HM: It's not mine.

NURSE: It's for the television.

HM: No it isn't.

NURSE: It changes the channels.

HM: You change the channels on the set.

NURSE: Ok well –

HM hands her the remote control.

HM: I want you to take this.

NURSE: Of course. Shall we do the…

She offers the newspaper to him.

HM: What's that?

NURSE: A crossword.

HM: Oh good!

NURSE: Good. Ok.

NURSE sits down next to him.

I'll read you the first one. District of Paris, home to the Sacré Coeur. Nine letters.

HM: Montmartre.

NURSE: You're so quick. How do you do it?

HM: You seem very familiar.

NURSE: Well Henry we have known. I have worked here a long time. Longer than I'd care to admit.

HM: Were we at school together? Now I know since the operation I have had trouble remembering things, but my school days, well, they seem to be in there somewhere, so maybe that's what it is. It was a while ago I guess, but it feels so close too. It's hard to tell sometimes isn't it?

NURSE: Yes.

HM: Maybe that's it. Maybe we were in the same class at school.

NURSE: Yes. Maybe that's it. Henry, do you… How old do you think you might be?

HM: I don't know if I. It would be hard to say, but I would maybe say my thirties… But you know. It's a funny thing isn't it?

NURSE: Mmm.

HM: But it certainly is nice to do things with people you know. Do a crossword.

NURSE: Watch a film.

HM: You like films?

NURSE: Oh yes. The classics.

HM: Well we could watch one together one day.

NURSE: I'd like that.

HM: Yes. It's nice to do things with someone you know isn't it?

NURSE: It is.
  I'll get you your breakfast.

HM looks in a mirror and sees the young HENRY on the other side.

13.

DR JACOPO ANNESE on-board an American Airlines flight from Boston to San Diego, 16 February 2009.

DR JACOPO ANNESE: So dinner was over, and we're cruising at, whatever, forty thousand feet. Only clouds below, and the horizon going on forever. That stage in the flight where people have made themselves at home.

Now you see it was on this flight that I started to make sense of the ideas I had had for a Brain Library. I'm surrounded by all these people – the old man asleep, snoring; the little girl kicking the chair in front of her. And I'm aware that I'm amongst this collection of incredible brains. We all hold that grey mass in a bone case inside our head, not much to look at but the amount going on...

I want to ask you to do something.

The lights slowly come up on the audience. A live feed projection of hands appears on the screen.

If you could put your hands in front of you so you are looking at your palms. Perfect. And now, if for a moment, you imagine that these are my hands. They are used to doing a lot of detailed work, you trust them.

Now if you close your eyes, and bring your hands towards you, so they rest on top of your head.

The projection goes dark as the hands are raised towards the camera and cover the lens as if following the instructions.

Your thumbs rest just on top of your ears, and the heel of your hand is sort of on your forehead. There you've got the idea.

And you can feel bone case underneath your hands. And under that, your brain. And inside that, Everything you've ever known. Everything you've ever experienced is somehow underneath your hands. And about five centimetres travelling straight in from where your thumbs are, is where your hippocampii live.

Imagine them there, two little seahorses, glowing deep in your brain. Sometimes referred to as a 'printing press'. The words I am saying right now are being sent there and printed into tiny 'books', memories, which will travel along the corridors of your brain to the cerebral cortex. The library. If Henry heard these words his brain would send them to the Hippocampus for printing, but of course there is nothing there. That information is sent to a dark gap.

Okay, now if you keep your eyes closed, you can let your hands come down to rest.

Now imagine Henry watching the trains go by. He stands at an open window. There is a gentle breeze. The smell of freshly cut grass. The hot sun on his face. He looks up and squints against the light. He smiles. He catches a glimpse of his reflection in the glass. He sees an old man, looking confused. The man wears dark thick rimmed glasses. Henry is searching for meaning in the picture he sees.

Now if you open your eyes.

HM is on a bare stage alone, looking searchingly at the audience.

You see Henry, Patient HM. There is a memory there. And then, that memory, is gone.

HM looks at the black. Whatever he was thinking has gone. He turns from the audience.

Blackout.

14.

There has been a silence, which is abruptly broken by the FATHER. The scene has the clipped mundane quality often found in clinical waiting rooms.

FATHER: He's a car man Dr Scoville, he likes them fast. But you know, classics. The engines. He's interested. You know what I mean Henry, the way you put it all together to make it go, I could never get my head around that, and your Mother!

MOTHER: No, no. I…

FATHER: But Dr Scoville. He has a whole fleet of cars I imagine. Wealthy Man. Discerning. Likes his cars, just like you.

HENRY: Yeah. I was thinking about going back to the garage.

FATHER: Yes.

HENRY: After the operation maybe. Get my old job back.

FATHER: You could son. You really could. It would be good for you. This is the start of something. We'll remember this day.

HENRY: Will you both be there after the operation?

MOTHER: Of course I will Henry.

FATHER: We both will. I'll be there. To see my son.

HENRY: I'm a bit scared.

MOTHER: Henry. You're the bravest man I know.

MOTHER holds HENRY's hands.

15.

Muffled voices are heard as HENRY goes under anaesthethic.

A physical choreographed sequence follows as the set swallows up MOTHER and FATHER.

HENRY is fighting to retain his memories, especially those of LAUREN. Familiar images from his memories are seen dissolving, burning, melting. Things disappear into the blackness. HENRY emerges from the operation as HM.

Muffled voices are heard again as HM comes round from the anaesthetic.

16.

HM stands close to the audience while behind him his MOTHER is revealed sitting as she was before the operation.

MOTHER: Henry.

HM: Yes.

MOTHER: You were mumbling.

HM: Was I?

MOTHER: Something about fishing.

HM: I'm always thinking about fishing, that's what you say isn't it you say I'm always thinking about fishing.

MOTHER: Well…

HM: Maybe when I'm out of here, I could go fishing with Dad.

MOTHER: Maybe.

HM: In the boat, sun on the lake, bright little speckles on the water.

MOTHER: You haven't been fishing with your Father for years.

HM: Oh.
   Where is he?

MOTHER: He's. He's not coming Henry. I told you.

HM: Did you?

MOTHER: Just a few minutes ago. I told you your Father is not here.

HM: Ok.

MOTHER: Henry. What's wrong with you?

HM: I don't know. I'm sorry.

MOTHER: No, no just… It's been weeks.

HM: Oh.

MOTHER: Since your operation.

HM: Yes. Weeks. Yes.

MOTHER: Henry please.

HM: What?

MOTHER: You're being –

HM: What?

MOTHER: I know they think there is something wrong with your memory but you, I mean you know I've been here don't you? You know I've been here everyday?

HM: Yes. Yes. That sounds right.

MOTHER: And you feel alright?

HM: Yes.

MOTHER: You feel healthy?

HM: Absolutely yes.

MOTHER: You're my Henry.

HM: Yes of course. Thank you for looking after me. You and Dad. Is he here?

Pause.

MOTHER: I don't know. I'll have a look.

MOTHER exits the room, she is seen in the corridor, she is overwhelmed and devastated. She breaks down. HM is alone in the room and looks out the window.

MOTHER takes a moment. She pulls herself together. In that moment she decides to give herself over to looking after HM for the rest of her life. She strides back into the room, HM is pleased to see her.

MOTHER: I had a look but I couldn't find him.

HM: Who?

MOTHER: Your Father.

HM: Oh.

MOTHER: You just asked me.

HM: Oh right.

MOTHER: It doesn't matter. I'm here Henry. I'll always be here.

17.

DR JACOPO ANNESE on-board an American Airlines flight from Boston to San Diego, 16 February 2009.

DR JACOPO ANNESE: We've been flying for almost four hours now, and my anxiety is replaced by anticipation. I feel ready. After all those years of training, carrying brains in cases on public transport, this moment feels almost inevitable. This is what it was all for. Henry and I flying together across America. I gave him the window seat.

I met him once before this flight. At the health centre, where he lived the last twenty-odd years of his life.

Macrotome movement to reveal NURSE and HM in his room. Chatting and watching the TV together.

It was not like Hollywood would make it, it was simple. He was very old. He had no idea that I was one of hundreds of scientists who had come to see him, or the time and effort it took to get to meet him. He just greeted me like anyone. I didn't have the opportunity to make a big connection, but I could see that kind demeanour, that smile. You could see why everyone liked him.

But they told me it was an ongoing struggle for all the staff not to treat him like a child or a pet. Not to patronise him.

'To Have and Have Not' is playing in the background.

MALE VOICE: *Walk around me. Go ahead walk around me. Clear around. You find anything?*

FEMALE VOICE: *No. No Steve there are not strings tied to you. Not yet. I liked that. Except for the beard. Why don't you shave and we'll try it again.*

HM: She loves this bit.

NURSE: Who?

HM: My mother.

NURSE: Really?

HM: Yes. She's a real romantic.

The NURSE smiles.

They watch for a while.

HM: Have you seen her, my mother? I'm having an argument with myself you see because I can't quite remember when I last saw her.

NURSE: …

H.M: Excuse me. I am talking to you. Do you know where my mother is? I can't remember when I last saw her. Where is she? Have you seen her? Has she been here?

HM becomes increasingly frustrated so the NURSE takes the remote control from her pocket and turns down the film.

NURSE: Henry, your mother died.
She died almost 11 years ago.
She died peacefully and she loved you very much.

HM breaks down and begins to cry. The NURSE has told him this before but still finds it difficult, she goes to comfort him and he shrugs her off. HM is agitated and continues to grow more and more distressed until the NURSE makes a decision to distract him.

NURSE: Hello Henry.

HM: Hello.

NURSE: Are you watching this film?

HM: Yes.

NURSE: I'll turn the volume up for you shall I? Now Henry, did you tell me a story about this film, that your Mother couldn't get the stove to work, so she said…

HM: Yes that's right. So she said 'Anybody got a match?'

NURSE: And it made your Father think of the film…

HM: Yes.

NURSE: Did he pretend to be, who is it?

HM: Humphrey Bogart. That's right.

NURSE: Swooped in like a real romantic lead.

HM: Yes exactly, and my Father took my Mother's hand, like this.

NURSE takes HM's hand, helps him out of his chair.

NURSE: Did he?

HM: And he spun her round the room.

NURSE: Really?

HM: Yes he spun her around and around and around and around…

They dance around the room as DR JACOPO begins to talk again.

DR JACOPO ANNESE: There was a photo of him on his bedroom wall.

The NURSE and HM exit. On the live feed we see a picture of HM.

And I sort of wish I had taken it. This photo of him as a young man, such a nice smile. I wanted to pluck it off the wall and you know, slip it into my jacket pocket. I wanted to know the person whose brain I was working with. That is the whole idea behind the Brain Library. I'm not interested in anonymous specimens in a bucket.

So now, I have a group of individuals who have offered their brains to my lab whom I meet regularly, for the interviews and tests but also, for dinner.

The actor playing DR JACOPO ANNESE leaves the microphone and sits on the stool, side on to the audience as if on the plane, with a large case containing between him and the audience as if sat by the plane window. As his final words increase in pace, the sound of a plane landing increases in volume and intensity.

We are beginning to descend and
the plane is a little choppy
nothing major
but still I sort of tighten my grip on the case
and as we near the ground
I look out the window
see the land below us
fields and buildings and roads.
I look at Henry, and out the window again
we are flying over a forest now
a great big green mass
hundreds of trees
millions of branches nestling together
connected but with space in between
and we come in closer and closer
and I think of zooming in on a single tree
and then on a single branch on that tree
and then on a single imperfection on that branch.

And the roar of the engine grows
we are about to land
Henry and I side by side

The case becomes translucent and HENRY's brain can be seen suspended inside.

The man who has taught the world so much
without ever knowing it
in the case under my hand.

And the wheels touch the ground and you feel the speed at which you have been travelling and I think what will you tell me now Henry? What will you tell the world next?

The Macrotome comes forward and swallows up everything on stage.

18.

'Once Upon A Time In The West' by Ennio Morricone is heard.

The Macrotome moves towards the audience, then returns to reveal the other two actors who turn to watch the screen. Words appear on the screen:

> On 2nd December 2009, over 53 hours, and watched live online by 400,000 people, Dr Jacopo Annese cut Henry Molaison's brain into slices.

> Henry became 2401 objects.

Recorded footage of HENRY's brain frozen in gelatine being cut into thin slices.

The actor playing DR JACOPO enters and takes off DR JACOPO's jacket at the lit microphone as if returning his voice to him. The recorded voice of DR JACOPO plays.

> I'm on again. Jacopo. Or Dr A is here again, to thank the performers and Analogue for creating this work surrounding the story of HM and his brain, and the procedure that sought to understand what happened to it.

> So you know that something has happened in your own brain, while you were watching this, and there are bits and pieces of the performance scattered all over your cerebral cortex, and every time you will think back of this performance, your hippocampus, your two hippocampii, will bring it all back together and make you relive it.

> In fact you the audience are part of this show. With your feedback you have modified the actor's brains.

> So there has been a lot of change neurologically speaking.

> And let's thank Henry for making us feel thankful for our intact and functioning hippocampus.

Good night.

The lights on stage go down. The projected footage remains for a short time before it too disappears.

Blackout.